How to Dazzle at

GRAMMAR

Irene Yates

Brilliant Publications

We hope you and your class enjoy using this book. Other books in the series include:

How to Dazzle at Writing	1 897675 45 3
How to Dazzle at Reading	1 897675 44 5
How to Dazzle at Spelling	1 897675 47 X
How to Dazzle at Reading for Meaning (available March 1999)	1 897675 51 8

If you would like further information on these or other titles published by Brilliant Publications, please write to the address given below.

Published by Brilliant Publications, The Old School Yard, Leighton Road, Northall, Dunstable, Bedfordshire LU6 2HA

Written by Irene Yates
Illustrated by Felicity House

Printed in Malta by Interprint Ltd

Contents

Introduction

How to Dazzle at Grammar contains 42 photocopiable sheets for use with pupils aged 8-13 who are working at Levels 1-3 of the National Curriculum (Scottish levels A-B). The activities are presented in an age-appropriate manner and provide a flexible but structured resource for teaching pupils to understand and use parts of speech and punctuation.

Because the concepts of syntax and punctuation are quite abstract, they are often difficult for pupils with special needs to assimilate. The concepts require reinforcement many times before they are understood. It is only when those concepts are understood that they become part of the pupils' own communication abilities. It is now widely believed that many children, particularly boys, who find English difficult to understand, actually have greater success with deconstructing and fragmenting language and learning how it 'works' in an analytical way with constant reinforcement than they do using it in a functional mode, through talking and writing.

Learning about grammar in this way gives the pupils the tools to be able to talk about and understand language development. Hopefully they then go on to make the knowledge they have acquired functional in their own communications but, of course, there is always the memory factor to take into account.

Part of the disaffection of pupils with special needs is the misery of failing time after time. The sheets are designed, with information and questioning, to help those pupils to experience success and achievement. The expectation that the pupil will achieve will help to build confidence and competence.

The tasks in the book are kept fairly short to facilitate concentration. The text on the pages is kept to a minimum, and the content of the pages is applied to contexts that the pupils will find motivating. In many cases there is an element of puzzle or competition to the activities to provide greater motivation. The extra task at the end of each activity provides reinforcement and enables pupils to use their skills in another way.

How to use the book

The activity pages are designed to supplement any English language activities you pursue in the classroom. They are intended to add to your pupils' knowledge of how the English language works.

They can be used with individual pupils, pairs or very small groups, as the need arises. The text on the pages has been kept as short as possible, so that reluctant or poorer readers will not feel swamped by 'words on the page'. For the same reason we have used white space and boxes, to help the pupils to understand the sheets easily, and to give them a measure of independence in working through them. In many instances, a pair of scissors and encouragement to 'cut and paste' will further help the pupils to work through the sheets.

It is not the author's intention that a teacher should expect all the pupils to complete all the sheets, rather that the sheets be used with a flexible approach, so that the book will provide a bank of resources that will meet needs as they arise.

Many of the sheets can be modified and extended in very simple ways. The Add-ons can provide a good vehicle for discussion of what has been learned and how it can be applied.

What is a proper sentence?

A proper **sentence** is a group of words that makes sense. A sentence can tell you something:

The clock ticks.	Boys like bikes.
Dinosaurs are extinct.	Dogs sleep.

Or it can ask a question:

Who won the match?	How much is the comic?

A proper sentence always begins with a capital letter and ends with a full stop, a question mark or an exclamation mark.

Write six proper sentences. Make three *tell* something and three *ask* a question.

1

2

3

4

5

6

Add-on
Write three proper sentences to answer your question ones.

Add some words

A group of words that doesn't make sense unless you add other words to it is not a sentence. It does not have to have a capital letter or a full stop.

Look at each group of words. Make them into proper sentences by adding more words. Write your sentence in the box.

number of ships

sentence

players on the field

sentence

when they are

sentence

not going

sentence

litter of puppies

sentence

go into the

sentence

off on a

sentence

is a band

sentence

Add-on
Turn three of your sentences into questions.

Simple sentences

Simple sentences have:

A subject	–	who or what is doing something
A verb	–	what the 'doing' is
An object	–	what or who the 'doing' is happening to

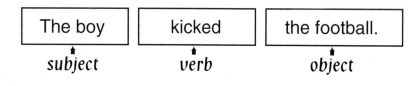

The boy	kicked	the football.
subject	*verb*	*object*

Pop stars	sing	songs.
subject	*verb*	*object*

Helpline
Remember to start each sentence with a capital letter and to end it with a full stop.

Write four simple sentences of your own. Give each sentence a subject, a verb and an object.

1

2

3

4

Add-on
Use a highlighter pen to highlight the subjects, verbs and objects in different colours.

Splitting the sentence

All sentences can be split into two parts. One part is the **subject** (the person, thing or place that the verb is about). The other part is the **predicate** (the rest of the sentence, containing the verb).

Subject	Predicate
The boy	kicked the ball into the net.
The ball	flew high over the goalpost.
The team	won the cup.
The game	was the best of the season.

Write predicates for these subjects.

Dinosaurs
The astronauts
Every rocket
All the pupils
The aliens

Write subjects for these predicates.

was hard work.
had great fun.
wanted to go on the roller coaster.
climbed up the tower.
roared.

Add-on
Find three sentences in your reading book and
split them into subjects and predicates.

Most important

The most important word (or words) in a sentence is the **verb**.
You can make a sentence out of just two words, using a subject and a verb:

Dogs dribble.

Athletes run.

Footballers train.

Aeroplanes fly.

Write four sentences of only two words.

1

2

3

4

Write four sentences of three words.

1

2

3

4

Add-on
Make sure there is a verb in each sentence.
Use a highlighter pen to highlight the verbs.

Writing verbs

A **verb** is a word that tells you what someone or something is doing.

**Write one verb to say what each of these animals might do.
(For example, how it might move.)**

More verbs

If a verb has the word 'to' in front of it, it is called an **infinitive**.

Here are some infinitive verbs:

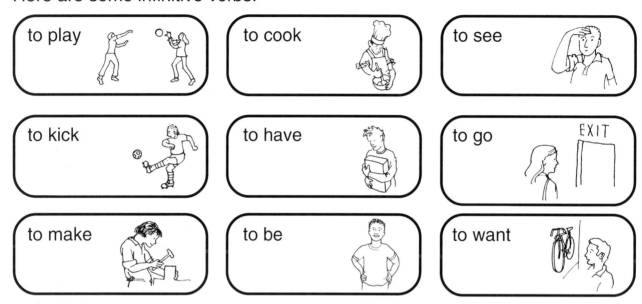

to play	to cook	to see
to kick	to have	to go
to make	to be	to want

Make a list of thirty infinitive verbs. There are thousands and thousands of verbs to choose from.

1	11	21
2	12	22
3	13	23
4	14	24
5	15	25
6	16	26
7	17	27
8	18	28
9	19	29
10	20	30

Add-on
Pick out four of your verbs and write a sentence for each one.

Pick out the verbs

Remember that verbs are 'doing' or 'being' words.

Draw a ring round the verbs in these sentences.

The dog wandered away.

The boy found the dog.

Where was the owner?

Who had lost the dog?

The boy didn't know what to do.

The dog sat.

Put verbs into these sentences to finish them.

The boy _____ the dog on a lead.

He _____ it from a bit of string in his pocket.

He _____ the dog home.

The dog _____ to be hungry.

It _____ a good wash and brush-up.

It must _____ to somebody, but who?

Add-on
Can you make up the rest of the story?
What happened next?

Getting the tense right

When you write a sentence, the verb has to be:

      in the present tense   –   Today I jump.

or, **in the past tense**   –   Yesterday I jumped.

or, **in the future tense**   –   Tomorrow I will jump.

Finish these sentences, getting the tenses right.

Helpline
All the words you put in must be verbs.

Yesterday, I _____ football.

Tomorrow, we _____ _____ training.

We _____ _____ in the semi-finals next month.

When we played Rovers, we _____ .

I _____ in the last match.

Our team _____ the greatest.

We _____ _____ a new strip next year.

Last week, I _____ captain.

Add-on
Write a story about your team.

Fill in the verb space

All the verbs have been missed out of this story. Read it carefully. Guess and write each verb in its box. Make sure the story is in the past tense.

For example: Chris went out. Jo said nothing.

Chris and Jo [   ] a dog. 'No,' [   ] Dad, 'but you [   ] [   ] a rabbit.'

A rabbit [   ] not what they [   ] . 'OK,' [   ] Dad. 'No pet.'

So, in the end, they [   ] .

On Saturday, they all [   ] to the market [   ] the rabbit. There [   ] hundreds. There [   ] all different kinds. The one they [   ] in love with [   ] an English Lop. It [   ] cream and honey-coloured. It [   ] long, floppy ears. 'We'll [   ] it Flop,' they [   ] .

Add-on
What do you think happened?
Write the next bit of the story.

How to Dazzle at Grammar

Changing the tense

Tense is about time. Something can happen *now* (the present), *yesterday* (the past) or *tomorrow* (the future).

The tense of verbs must always be correct.

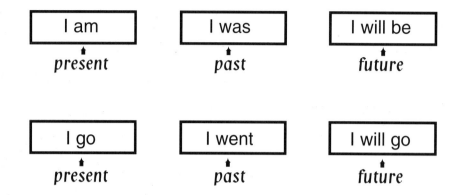

Write these verbs in their different tenses:

	present	past	future
to want	I _____	I _____	I _____
to play	He _____	He _____	He _____
to see	We _____	We _____	We _____
to buy	They _____	They _____	They _____
to swim	I _____	I _____	I _____
to have	We _____	We _____	We _____

Add-on
Choose one verb and write three
different sentences for it.

Yesterday ...

This story is written as if it is happening now. But it really happened yesterday. Read it carefully. Write it again, putting it in the past tense.

The Badger Rescue

Today I feel good. I go to visit my mate. He has a new bike. We fetch my bike and go off for a ride in the woods. We feel really good. Then something happens. We hear a noise in the bushes. We leave our bikes to find out what it is. The noise sounds like a little animal. It is crying. We push our way through the bushes. We find a baby badger that is hurt. We have to save it.

Write the story in the past tense here:

Helpline
Think about the verbs.

Add-on
What do you think happens next?

Today ...

This story is written as though it happened yesterday. But it is really happening right now. Read it carefully. Write it again, putting it in the present tense.

The Aliens Have Landed

Ben went into the garden. There was something funny there. The apple tree had gone. In its place was a huge, round object with lots of flashing lights. It was a UFO. Aliens had landed in the garden! 'Wow!' thought Ben. He went up to the little hatch on the front of the spaceship. He knocked. Ben wasn't scared of aliens!

Write the story in the present tense here:

Helpline
Think about the verbs.

Add-on
What do you think happens next?

Describe it ...

The words that tell you what someone, or something, is like are called **adjectives**.

Adjectives **describe**.

Here is a dinosaur.

Find six words that describe it.

1 _____

2 _____

3 _____

4 _____

5 _____

6 _____

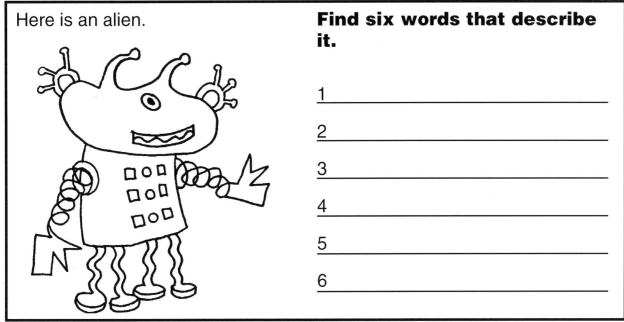

Here is an alien.

Find six words that describe it.

1 _____

2 _____

3 _____

4 _____

5 _____

6 _____

Add-on
Find six words to describe your best friend.
Check your spellings in a dictionary.

Writing adjectives

An **adjective** is a word that tells you what someone, or something, is like. It **describes**.

Write one adjective to describe each of these things:

Add-on
Choose one of the animals.
Write a paragraph about it.

What's he like?

Adjectives can tell you what somebody or something looks like.

Find six adjectives for each of the boxes. Try not to use the same word twice.

Your favourite footballer	
1	4
2	5
3	6

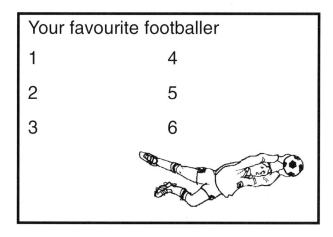

Your favourite pop star	
1	4
2	5
3	6

A Harley Davidson motorcycle	
1	4
2	5
3	6

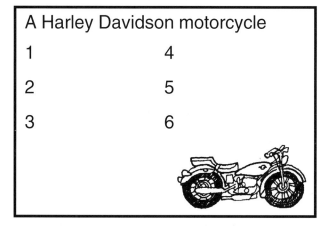

A mountain bike	
1	4
2	5
3	6

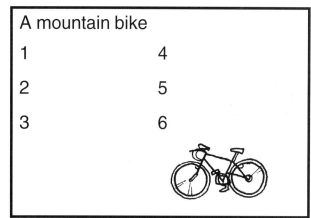

Your favourite food	
1	4
2	5
3	6

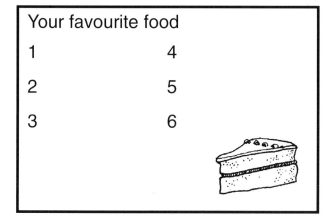

Your classroom	
1	4
2	5
3	6

Add-on
Write six adjectives to describe someone or something.
Get a friend to guess what you are describing.

Adding adjectives

You can add **adjectives** to simple sentences. Adjectives are words that describe. They tell you what something is like.

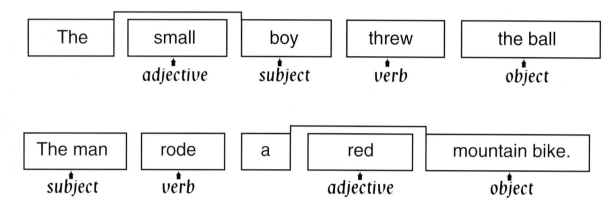

The	small	boy	threw	the ball
	adjective	*subject*	*verb*	*object*

The man	rode	a	red	mountain bike.
subject	*verb*		*adjective*	*object*

Write four simple sentences of your own, using an adjective in each one.

1

2

3

4

Add-on
Use a highlighter pen to highlight all the adjectives
in your sentences.

Now for nouns

The words that give things **names** are called **nouns**.

Write the nouns for these things:

© Irene Yates
This page may be photocopied for use by the purchasing institution only.

How to Dazzle at Grammar

Guess-the-noun

Nouns are the names of things.

Write the correct noun for each picture in the box.

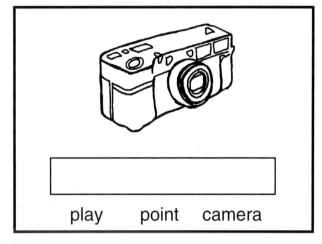

play   point   camera

trainers   try   run

eat   hungry   burger

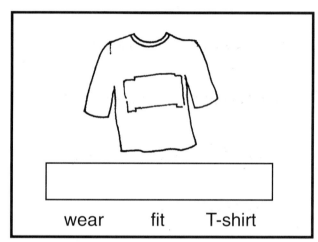

wear   fit   T-shirt

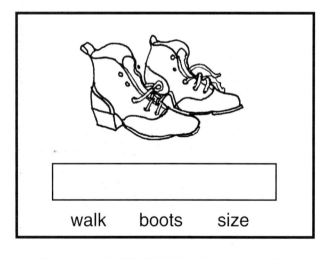

walk   boots   size

read   books   words

Add-on
Write a sentence using at least two of these nouns.

How many nouns?

Remember that **nouns** are words that are the **names** of things:

astronaut   athlete   computer

Use a highlighter pen to highlight the nouns in this story.

Helpline
There are 10 nouns.

The boys collected four old lawnmowers in the shed. They

stripped the engines out of them. They fixed the engines into the

karts. After lining up the karts, they turned the switches, laughing.

To their amazement, the engines started up and off they sped,

along the track … !

Add-on
Write what happened next.

What's your name?

Nouns that are somebody's real name are called **proper nouns**.
They have to begin with a capital letter.

Neil

Inderjit

Mr Wood

Emma

Mabel

Make a list of proper nouns you know.
Start with your own name.

1	6	11
2	7	12
3	8	13
4	9	14
5	10	15

The days of the week are proper nouns. Write them here:

M _____

T _____

W _____

T _____

F _____

S _____

S _____

Add-on
Check your spellings of the days of the week,
with a dictionary.

How does it go?

You can use **adverbs** in simple sentences. An adverb tells you **how** something is happening.

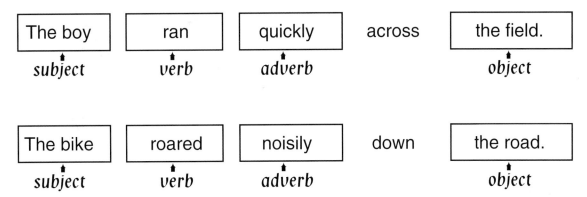

| The boy | ran | quickly | across | the field. |
| subject | verb | adverb | | object |

| The bike | roared | noisily | down | the road. |
| subject | verb | adverb | | object |

Write four sentences of your own, using an adverb in each one.

Helpline
Lots of adverbs end in 'ly'.

1

2

3

4

Add-on
Use a highlighter pen to highlight
the adverbs in your sentences.

Pronouns

Pronouns are the words we sometimes use to make verbs work.
They save us using nouns all the time. The pronouns are:

	verb to be	verb to have
I	I am	I have
You	You are	You have
He	He is	He has
She	She is	She has
It	It is	It has
We	We are	We have
They	They are	They have

Change these verbs to fit the pronouns:

	verb to sing	verb to want	verb to eat
I	_____	_____	_____
You	_____	_____	_____
He	_____	_____	_____
She	_____	_____	_____
It	_____	_____	_____
We	_____	_____	_____
They	_____	_____	_____

Add-on
Write one sentence for each pronoun,
choosing your own verbs.

Preposition wordsearch

Prepositions are usually little words. They are the words that show how one thing relates to another.

For example:

She went **to** the door.
He rushed **into** the house.
They walked **across** the room.

Find these prepositions in the wordsearch. They can be up, down, across or diagonal.

with	in	on	at	to
up	down	into	after	for
of	from	between		

b	w	f	r	o	m	r	k
n	e	p	j	u	n	e	i
y	x	t	b	p	i	t	n
o	n	c	w	q	d	f	t
d	o	w	n	e	m	a	o
a	t	f	o	r	e	x	o
w	i	t	h	k	r	n	t

Add-on
Write a sentence for each preposition you find.

Means the same

Lots of words look and sound different, but mean almost the same thing.

Draw lines to match the words that mean the same in these lists.

difficult   huge

little   lots

big   speak

jump   hard

many   jog

name   spring

say   nasty

run   small

horrible   ancient

old   noun

Write a word that means the same as:

scared   _____

nice   _____

tired   _____

give   _____

Add-on
Words that mean the same are called **synonyms**.
Practise writing and saying this word.
Write a sentence explaining what a synonym is.

Means something different

Many words have opposites.

Draw lines to match the words which are opposites in these lists.

love	open
dry	awake
close	found
night	wet
asleep	answer
lost	hate
rich	day
thin	new
question	fat
old	poor

Write a word which is the opposite of:

easy _____

far _____

wild _____

right _____

Add-on
Words that mean the opposite are called **antonyms**.
Practise writing and saying this word.
Write a sentence explaining what an antonym is.

Idioms

Idioms are expressions we use to make our language more colourful.

Here are some examples:

saved by the bell

catch my breath

cloud cuckoo land

as dead as a dodo

Write a sentence that uses each of these idioms:

idiom	sentence
big deal	_____
down to earth	_____
in the long run	_____
look snappy	_____
sit tight	_____
a bad penny	_____

Add-on
Make a list of six more idioms that you know and use.

What do you know about the alphabet?

How many letters are there in the alphabet? _____

Write the small letters:

a   b   c   d

Write the letters in capitals:

A   B   C   D

What is the fifth letter of the alphabet? _____

Which letter is seventh from the end? _____

Which letter comes before i? _____

Which letter comes after Q? _____

Which letter is tenth from the end? _____

Which is the twentieth letter? _____

Add-on

Put these groups of letters into the right order:

BCA   LKJ   TSU   ONP   YWX

_____   _____   _____   _____   _____

Alphabet code

This is the alphabet in the correct order.

a	b	c	d	e	f	g	h	i	j	k	l	m
b	*c*	*d*										

n	o	p	q	r	s	t	u	v	w	x	y	z

Write the alphabet again in the boxes underneath, but move the letters one space back.

Now you have a code. Here are some words written in the code:

eph means *dog*   cjlf means   *bike*

Write your name in code:

Write your friend's name in code:

Opx ep zpvs pxo xpset:

Write a secret message to your friend:

Add-on
Make a new code. First write the alphabet out normally. Then, underneath, write it backwards, beginning with putting **z** under **a**.

Alphabetical order

Words are often written in the order of the alphabet. This makes it easier to look for them in a dictionary.

These words are in alphabetical order because their first letters come after each other in the alphabet.

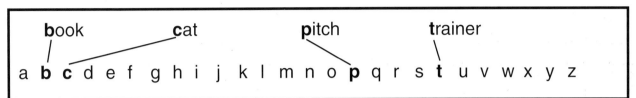

| book | cat | pitch | trainer |

a **b c** d e f g h i j k l m n o **p** q r s **t** u v w x y z

---

Arrange these words in alphabetical order:

ice	Monday	June	baby	was
socks	coat	grass	ear	letter
and	pop	disco	new	on

Add-on
Write a sentence using three of the words in alphabetical order.

The right order

Remember the alphabet?

Write the alphabet in the correct order here using capital letters:

A   B   C

Put these names of people and places into alphabetical order:

Helpline
Notice that all these words begin with capital letters.

China	Ohio	Vernow	Birmingham	
Donna	Xian	Yasmin	Jack	
Harry	Nigel	William	Eric	
Pat	Una	Fred	India	Tasmania
Simon	Ken	Ryan	Gail	Majorca
Asia	Queenie	Les	Zambia	

Add-on
Make your own alphabetical list of names.

What's wrong?

Can you see what is wrong with Ben's project? It's not in proper sentences. He hasn't put in the **full stops** and **capital letters**.

Find the eight missing capital letters and eight missing full stops.

lots of wild animals live in towns you can find them in your garden if you look hard enough birds look for good places to build their nests they like thick shrubs and trees insects like lots of wild flowers piles of dead leaves make homes for insects butterflies love plants that produce lots of nectar you can easily make good habitats for wild life

Write Ben's project out again, putting in the missing capital letters and full stops.

Add-on
Write a sentence saying why full stops and capital letters are useful.

Ask for an answer

When you write a sentence that *asks* something, it is a **question**. A sentence that is a question must have a **question mark** at the end of it, instead of a full stop.

This is a question mark: **?**

Write a line of question marks here:

Look at the pictures:

Write some questions about the pictures.

Who _____

What _____

Why _____

When _____

Where _____

How _____

> *Helpline*
> Don't forget the question marks.

Add-on
Get a friend to write answers to your questions.

Question quiz

Read the sentences in the boxes. Put question marks at the end of the sentences which are questions. Put full stops at the end of the sentences that are not.

What is your favourite team game

My bike is the latest model

Do you like athletics

I love pop music

Who is your favourite player

Have you been in an aeroplane

Tyrannosaurus rex was huge

My favourite subject is art

Can you draw well

What is your favourite animal

I love dogs

Add-on
Write sentences to answer each of the questions.

Asking questions

A **question** is a sentence that asks something. It always ends with a **question mark** (?) instead of a full stop.

Look at these mini-beasts:

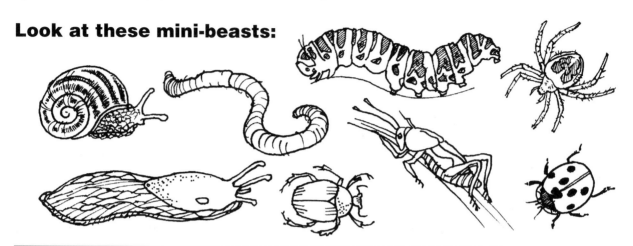

Write eight questions that will help you find out the differences between them. Don't forget the question marks.

An example might be: Does it have wings?

1 _____

2 _____

3 _____

4 _____

5 _____

6 _____

7 _____

8 _____

Add-on
Write a paragraph about mini-beasts.

Speech marks

When you write a story and someone speaks, you have to use **speech marks** like this:

'Oh!' he said.

'Why?' she asked.

'I come from the planet Zog,' said the alien.

Inside the speech marks the words must begin with a capital letter and end with a punctuation mark.

Put the speech marks and punctuation marks into these speeches:

i'm going to town Jo's mum said

do you want to come with me

no said Jo

it's pouring with rain

that doesn't matter mum said

we'll go in the car

I think not said Jo

it's got a flat tyre

Add-on
Write down the next thing someone says to you
and put it in speech marks.

Commas in lists

One of the jobs of a **comma** is to help with the writing of lists. Where there is a list of words in a sentence, each word in the list is separated from the next by a comma.

For example:

> We will need a saw, hammer and nails.
>
> Bob is a friendly, cheerful boy.
>
> Sam teases the cat, frightens the dog and bullies his brother.

Put commas in these lists:

The dinosaur was huge frightening and hungry.

It roared groaned and grunted.

Everyone screamed shrieked and ran for cover.

The dinosaur raised its small bony head and looked.

They had laser guns spears and javelins but nothing could turn it away.

Add-on
Write another sentence with a list.
Don't forget to add the commas.

All mixed up

These words are all adjectives, nouns or verbs. They are all mixed up. Put them in their right places.

dip	long	spawn	swim
tiny	collect	pond	move
tadpole	murky	weedy	fishing net
frog	draw	wet	surface
quiet	investigate	water	find

adjectives

nouns

Helpline
Watch out!
Some words
will fit into more
than one box.

verbs

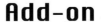

Add-on
Write three sentences about a pond-dipping experiment.

The pet dog puzzle

This puzzle tells you something about looking after a dog.
The words are all in the wrong order.

Helpline
There are five sentences.

Cut out the words and shuffle them around to work out the sentences. Write the sentences on the sheet.

Dogs	them	meat,	need	exercise.	pets.
is	Take	They	plenty	Feed	for
and	vegetables	make	a	good	them
walks	make	of	on	and	attention
Always	very	of	twice	day.	biscuits.
sure	water	clean	lots	there	drinking.

Dogs make

Add-on
Do you know any more tips for looking after dogs?

The fabulous football match puzzle

This puzzle tells you something about a fabulous football match. The words are all in the wrong order.

Helpline
There are eight sentences.

Cut out the words and shuffle them around to work out the sentences. Write the sentences on the sheet.

It	the	He	felt	minutes	his
meant	headed	Three	cup	huge	The
took	was	Suddenly	it	to	leap.
a	way.	desperate.	go.	ball	He
everything	net.	straight	Goal!	the	him.
two	Daz	came	into	to	all.

Three minutes

Add-on
Write a story about the best goal you ever scored or saw.

The owl puzzle

This is information about owls. The words are all in the wrong order.

Cut out the words and shuffle them around to work out the sentences. Write the sentences on the sheet.

Helpline
There are five sentences.

Owls	Each	glide,	the	hunters.	thing
important	their	are	voles	are	and
silent	brilliant	They	Food	They	catches
every	dark.	thousands	grab	is	flying.
most	surprise	owl	year.	when	prey
the	life.	in	in	of	their

Owls are

Add-on
Write two more sentences about owls.

The running champion puzzle

This puzzle is a story about a running champion called Sam. The words are all in the wrong order.

Helpline
There are five sentences.

Cut out the words and shuffle them around to work out the sentences. Write the sentences on the sheet.

Sam	He	and	running.	He	champion.
run	was	He	England.	knew	be
good	to	at	got	Sam	for
that	ran	one	day.	day	faster.
every	faster	he	would	wanted	a

Sam was

Add-on
Write two more sentences about Sam.

Check what you know

The different words we use are called **parts of speech**.

Draw lines to match each part of speech with the job it does in a sentence.

verb	a small word
adjective	tells you how
pronoun	tells you what something is like
adverb	tells you what is happening
preposition	names something
noun	replaces a noun

Write two words for each part of speech:

verb _____ _____

adjective _____ _____

noun _____ _____

adverb _____ _____

preposition _____ _____

pronoun _____ _____

Add-on
Can you make up a sentence using each
part of speech once?